YOU CAN CHANGE YOUR STORY

There Are No Awards for Suffering™

Susan Annette

Table of Contents

INTRODUCTION:

One day I was up early, sitting having my morning coffee and reflecting, and I thought to myself "why didn't I just say what I wanted to the love of my life, why didn't I just say that I didn't feel love?" I wanted him to spend some time with me; a holiday. Why didn't I just say it and then when he changed the subject, why didn't I say it again? Why did it take me so long to realize that if I required something, be it love, time, honesty, etc, Why didn't I just ask? Why did I set others up for failure? By thinking they could read my mind that they would know what I needed? Most importantly, if I was really loved, WE would do things that made US happy, not just them. As equals.

When I would try to voice my needs, I would get deflection. Then I would just take that personally and stop asking all together. I would just begin hurting inside and suffering silently, like there was some award for that.

What was I thinking? I was thinking constantly how sorry I felt for me, for being alone, for not feeling loved, OMG is that what I was really thinking? Yes, unfortunately it was. Which is even sadder than not feeling loved, because I HAD the POWER to change all of that with my thoughts and my story.

This was a huge awakening and even bigger was that I realized my trainer had everything to do with this and my long, suffering life. I was trained to suffer, trained from the very beginning that my thoughts and needs were not important to anyone else. While that could certainly be true, they are important to me. I should be able to voice my needs. I've seen people do it and get what they want. Women and men. Why wasn't I getting what I needed? I innocently thought, though suffering in silence, was noble. Holy cow, what a misconception I had in my head.

It was that morning so long ago, that moment that I realized "There are no Awards for Suffering". Not one single trophy, acknowledgement, no Nobel Peace Prizes, no publications, nothing ever mentioned anywhere. There are no Awards for Suffering? Really? I have suffered all these years making everyone else fulfill their dreams and I silently fumed, suffered, felt sorry for myself, and yet not one award. Worse yet I suffered in silence so nobody even knew I was suffering. I talked to myself about it constantly at night when I should have been sleeping, or at work during the day, and even when I was walking to ease the stress. All that time, I was talking to myself about all the suffering and how I didn't feel loved.

Every relationship I had was based on me fixing them. My husband had lost all his money in a previous divorce and our relationship was forged in a deal that I would help him make his retirement. In return he would be the "best old man I ever had". He Lied. My next relationship I was going to be everything he needed and had done without in his whole life. I was, and not one time, did we discuss what I needed. Not once. The 3rd relationship I was going to be the health guru; exercise, food, supplements. I was bringing him back to his healthy self and we would live happily ever after. Once that was done, I said to myself, "Now what will I do, he's healthy and ready for a future, what is my purpose now?"

In all those relationships, I did not feel loved. I felt alone. Even though I did all the things I said I would do, I felt left out of their lives. Most of all, I didn't know that I should be asking for what I wanted. I set them all up for failure. I broke my own heart and I am the reason I didn't feel loved. It wasn't their job to fix me, it wasn't mine to fix them.

Then one day, I figured out that I should love myself like I want to be loved. Totally, unconditionally, and without judgment. Most of all, I don't have to fix or repair anyone else or their life. I broke my own heart by being in relationships that were one sided. Not with my own best interest at heart.

I had been silently living my life letting people walk all over me and I realized that nobody cares how much you suffer. It was in this that I started my journey in finding out who I was and how to love myself. I promised myself that I was going to love me like I wanted to be loved. Unconditionally to not have to perform for that love. But to just simply be loved for who I was. I wasn't going to let anyone else break my heart again but more importantly I made the commitment that I was never going to break my own heart again.

I am responsible for my story, my life, and the love I require, and I had the power not to break my own heart. No one else has that power, only me. I have the power to love me like I need to be loved and I have the power to love someone else who is whole on their own, not broken, not unhealthy. I can control myself, my destiny, and my future with my story.

You Can Change Your Story Too.

Permission to: Change Your Story

When I was in the 1st grade our teacher went around the room and asked us what we wanted to be when we grew up. At 6 I had no idea really, I just knew I wanted to own my own business, no idea what that was though. How could I say that? I was too shy and timid. So, I said whatever the last girl said that sounded good. Maybe a teacher or a nurse. I don't really know. That was my story.

When I was growing up, until my first husband came around, I lived with the most physically abusive man I had ever met. He wasn't my real dad, but he made me the worker bee. I was in charge of 3 other children; a family of 6. I was the family caretaker, nurse, nanny, cleaner, ironing lady, all the things a maid would do. I was the girl who was in charge of everything so everyone else could live. If I didn't do them perfectly, there was hell to pay. I lived my life in fear of the next beating. I didn't know everyone didn't live this way, that this wasn't how others raised their children; the oldest child living like a maid. I was living in a fairy tale and didn't even know it; I was Cinderella. That was my story.

When my mom was 40 she got diagnosed with Cancer, 18 months later she was gone. That was my story.

One day just before I turned 38 I met the most handsome man who was amazing, kind and gentle and treated me like a queen. All I had to do was help him make back his retirement and he promised he would be the best old man I ever had. I believed him. I worked 7 days a week with him. We built a business and lifestyle that stopped me from seeing my family on holidays or birthdays. We would only see his family. I did everything he wanted because I loved him. He made sure I had anything I desired. Cars, jewelry, a beautiful home, I was the Queen Bee and everyone wanted to be me. It was everything I dreamed for my life. Total success, I thought.

Everyone thought we had a perfect life when viewed from the outside of the relationship. Seen from within, I was so lonely and I didn't know why. I loved him so much and I adored him and we did everything we set out to do. We made his retirement, built his perfect dream shop, and had 4 successful businesses. But I was always alone. He did always come home every night, we had dinner together, he did everything he said, but I was just so alone and couldn't figure out why!

One day I had a feeling that he wasn't being honest about where he was. It was intuition that made me go to the employee files and look up our secretary's address. I locked the front door of our business and got into my car and drove to her home which was only 2 miles away. There, outside of her home, was his truck and her car. My heart fell and I suddenly knew why I was so alone. I also knew that my whole life was a lie. Everything he told me, convinced me to do for him, it was all a lie. When I confronted him, he lied more and when I told him our deal, he said he would walk away if he didn't do right by me, he said 2 words that put it all in perspective.

"I lied." he said.

Those were his words, but he wouldn't walk away. The best part was I never felt a second of jealousy which was a huge gift. I guess I knew the whole time he was lying. That was my story.

For 14 long years that was my story, I struggled to find myself, to understand. I thought about it every day, every way I could. Then one day I said, "I need help, I can't be this girl anymore or I will die right

here, right now. I need peace, love and help."
So, I started reading books, taking seminars,
learned a new business, anything to keep
busy and grow myself. I still had this story
all that time, I called it the train wreck. The
5-minute train wreck from the movie *The
Fugitive*, it was devastating to me.

Then one day, 14 long years later, I realized
I had created another life. One full of
friends, love for myself and many things I
desired. Why would I still have the train
wreck for my story? Why not change my
story to one full of hope and living? Why be
bogged down with that same old story? And
just like that, I had a beautiful story of love
for myself, good friends who love me just as
I am, no back biting, and no competition.
Just beautiful people who care about others
like I do. Family weekends all at my home
full of love and great times. Everything I
dreamed my life could be. I created it myself
by thinking I could and making the small
steps toward it until they became giant

steps and my reality. Wow, now that's a story.

The main idea I am trying to make is that your story changes as you do. If people get stuck in the same story for a whole lifetime they are not living. Your story should always be changing. One day it should be a fairy tale with a happily ever after.

You Can Change Your Story™

Whether you realize it or not, you can change your story. Many of us have stories that we live by, some of those are good stories, and many of them are not. Maybe the current story of your life is about abuse that you've suffered, maybe it's about rejection from people, or you've lost a loved one. All of those stories that we base our lives on, have an impact on how we live our life but the thing that we often are not told, the simple truth, is that you can change your story. The universe is love. It is meant for you to love and to be loved and today is your day to step away from what is or was in the past and change your story.

I have been told by many people I have a really big heart. What I can say to that is it has been broken many times. I grew up next door to my grandmother whose heart was as big as Texas. She taught me about love, loving others and giving. If she had two of something, she would always divide with you. One for you, one for her. I believe she taught me there was really love and compassion in this life.

Growing up in a family with 4 children (me being the oldest) and a father with an iron hand, the only love and compassion I ever felt was from my grandmother. She was my light, my savior, my peace when the battle was too big for a little girl to handle, too much weight on my shoulders to bear. Her words of encouragement would keep me going. Perception is everything.

When I was growing up as a real-life Cinderella I thought, being the oldest of 4 children, I was responsible for everything. I didn't know any different, there wasn't anyone to tell me any difference. As a result, I wasn't angry or feeling sorry for myself. I was stressed by all the responsibility for which I wasn't prepared for. Babysitting 3 kids when you are still a kid yourself is a big order. The discipline my father instilled in me, turned out to be something I used in everything I did and became.

Successful in many different businesses, even when others lost everything in the downturn in the 90's, I had already prepared for it by paying everything off, and holding on to my money. It was 10 long years before the economy would return to its former glory. I used this time to buy another business I knew nothing about, learn everything I could about it and change it into a company with a big heart that would help others in need who were alone.

Then, Beach Organics was born. I created bath and body products with a mission. In my research I learned that if you can use products without chemicals you can improve your immune system which fights diseases and especially cancer cells. I would take the profits and give them to Cancer patients who lost their jobs, and couldn't pay electric bills or buy groceries. I would align myself with organization who helped these people and I would let them know they are not alone in the battle. By helping them, I could fulfill my mother's dream of helping people.

I grew into a person with a heart for others, I had compassion for those less fortunate who couldn't see the exit from their current situation. In my own dark times I just wished I knew the secret word, the thing that would bring me peace from the terror I sometimes felt. A word that once spoken could put all the pieces of my broken heart back together again so I could be whole. It would be years before I would know it really wasn't a word, but 5 words. Five words that would give me peace and a new thought pattern that would lead to relief and love. Love for myself and love for others. Five words that would give me so much peace and enlightenment, that everyone I shared them with saw the same light I did. Five little words that they could use to change their life too.

It is within our power to control our life, our thoughts. We can choose happiness or sadness like a stop light. One minute it is red the next it is green. When it turns yellow you pause and re align yourself with you and make the choice to love. To love yourself. These 5 words may not mean anything to you yet, and you're probably asking yourself, "What?" Don't limit yourself to just the questions, listen first, then you will see it is the magic words: You Can Change Your Story™.

Today I have an amazing successful life and I own a couple of different businesses. I have truly amazing friends; we do fun things together. We laugh, we joke, we enjoy being in each other's company. I'm proud to be able to say that I support many charities. I spend my time now creating the life that I always wanted. I like to dress up and meet lots of people and know that the work that I'm doing makes a difference. I was fortunate enough to build the house that I now live in, this is the dream house that I've always wanted. I'm living the life filled with all of the things that I ever imagined doing. Most importantly, I've learned how to love myself unconditionally. I don't tell you this to brag about how great my life is, but rather to paint for you the picture that my life is now, compared to the way my life used to be.

I was born and raised in North Carolina, the oldest of my brother and 2 sisters and as a friend of mine once said, *Cinderella* in my childhood home. My opinion was never considered and I had a father, who was not hateful or mean, but he was very forceful and he believed that beating a child, bringing them into order and having them live in an absolute perfected state, deeply disciplined with no room for error, he believed that was right. Of course, as a flawed human being, I got beaten many times when I did things wrong. I felt that was how everybody was brought up. As a child I believed that that's just what childhood was. Or should I say, maybe I didn't have a childhood, but simply that was just the job that I worked.

Behind every successful person there is always a story to share. Sometimes you won't even believe the story because you see the person *after* they've become successful. That's not the true picture, take me for example; my story, I really didn't even know it was a story until much later in life when someone pointed it out to me.

I grew up very poor in rural North Carolina. My parents were hard working, god fearing people who had 4 children, a house payment, 2 cars and a lot on their plates. Work weeks were 50 hours a week, so you could make that overtime. When they were at home, they were tired. Six days a week, getting up at 5:00 am to get ready for the work day and home at 5:00 pm to have supper, relax a little, and then back to bed for the next day. That didn't leave much time for children or patience for young children.

As a result, we all had our jobs to do. Each day, that included cleaning the house, making beds, sweeping the floors from all the dirt 6 people can drag into a house. Of course, me being the oldest, I had a lot more responsibility. It was my responsibility to make sure the other 3 children of the household were doing their jobs. Then I was to cook dinner and have it ready each evening for when my parents would come home.

I was young myself and made a lot of mistakes, like trying to cook lettuce for cabbage. I could never tell the difference. Or not cooking the chicken long enough. I was a child myself, how was I supposed to know? Those mistakes were costly, just like if I washed the dishes and there was a speck of food left on one by mistake upon inspection, I got to wash them ALL over again. Though this was annoying, it gave me the grounding to make sure things were done right, to have discipline to do things like they should be.

I didn't know any better, so I did what I was told. My opinion was never acknowledged, I had no value in our household except, of course, baby sitter, cook, and maid. Those were my jobs for as long as I could remember. It was very stressful looking after and dealing with my siblings, and often times I would confide in my grandmother that I may have a nervous breakdown. I didn't really know what that was at 9, but I had heard my mom say it many times, so I thought maybe I would have that also if those kids didn't straighten up. It was a big weight being the go-to for everyone.

While all of that seems like a lot, there is one thing I haven't gone too far into. My dad ruled with an iron hand. He was thin man, very quiet who loved to watch TV. Especially sports. Any sport and every sport. His idea of babysitting was lining us up on the sofa across from him and for hours we watched football, basketball, wrestling, softball, baseball, any sport that was on TV. The thing is, we weren't allowed to say anything, just be quiet and watch hours of people including him cheering and yelling.

If we needed to go to the bathroom we could ask and he would approve or deny the movement. If we found ourselves in trouble, it was a discipline that sadly, some of you can relate with.

My father would line all 4 of us up and question us each on who had committed the crime, whatever it was, with a belt in hand. He'd ask the first one in line and if the answer was wrong he would start the spanking with the belt and you were not allowed to cry. Then the next one down the line and all the way to end which was usually me, holding back the tears. If you cried, you got it worse. Discipline my love, you had to be strong. Don't cry no matter how painful, how many stripes you had on your legs. No tears were allowed.

I had been taught by the best from the time I could walk that you have to be stoic or the penalty would be almost unbearable. I came out of this alive and with the battle scars across my body. Permanently bruised and scarred from the beatings. Hidden so no one could see the pain I endured, hidden deep inside sometimes shaking all over, red faced and scared to death, but no crying was allowed. Here's the thing, it didn't stop me, it just pushed me harder.

All of this, instilled in me some good things, things like discipline. I was trained to be a disciplined individual and I learned how to be in service to other people. From as little as six years old, I knew that I was going to be in business, even though back then I didn't know what that meant. I'm grateful for those things that I did learn, in spite of how I learned them. I moved away from home and as a young adult I took that story into my adulthood. Did he intend to hurt me? No way, it's just he didn't know any better, he only knew what he was taught.

As a young lady, at the age of 24 years old, my mom got sick with cancer. I would have given anything to save her. I wanted for me to be the one to die instead of her. I knew that her ultimate goal was to be of service to people and I feel honored to be a tribute to her through the things that I do to help others. I started my own business and it was successful because of the discipline that I had learned in my childhood. The discipline worked for me and I found that the discipline carried forward into my work.

While my mother was sick, we spent the last 2 months in the hospital. It was 18 months from the time she was diagnosed until she passed. To say it was a heart wrenching 18 months is an understatement. I was really young and back then very few people had cancer. I read everything I could find in the hospitals (no internet back then). I silently watched people going in and out of radiation. She got really sick from it and couldn't work anymore. We didn't have money so she had to stand in lines to receive unemployment, which in itself, was degrading. Every day I was with her from early morning to late evening. One of the things she said was she didn't want to die and if she could live she would help people. Through all the tough times we weren't used to asking for help. People back then just didn't file for unemployment. Then her health insurance was canceled because she couldn't work anymore.

I remember the morning I got up, dressed in my best clothing at the time, went to the place she had worked 22 years and where I had summer jobs. The plant was a block long and the owner was a very important person. I begged him to please have mercy on us, we couldn't pay the $20.00 a month co-pay. There just wasn't any money, she couldn't work and I spent my time as her caregiver and support system. He agreed. It was a world changing time for us, she could continue treatment. That was one of many battles I would fight for her, or rather stand up for her. I told this story at a cancer gathering and everyone cried with me. To this day more than 30 years later I cry when telling this story of being a gladiator for my mother.

I really thought she may make it through this. I silently prayed to God to take me instead, to let her live. Nobody would really miss me after all, and I didn't have purpose or meaning to my life at the time. I was 26 and really didn't have a direction. It didn't happen. She didn't live. At 42 her life was over. I was devastated. She was my life line, my everything.

I decided the day she passed, if I could ever make enough money I would help people in her honor. I didn't know how or when, I just knew that was my grounding, my passion, my purpose. That day in the hospital set my whole future, however convoluted it would become, ultimately, I would fulfill her passion and make it my own.

The whole lesson in this is I help people that I will never meet, I will never know. I give money, products and I support them. I sell to the public, on amazon and health food stores across the nation. All this because of one statement my beautiful dying mother said to me one day alone in a hospital room. It touched my heart and soul and gave me the passion to believe in myself. I'm not a chemist, I am just a girl who loved her mother. It took me 30 years to say out loud "my mother passed". It broke my heart. She lives in me and I am fulfilling her dream and mine of helping people in ways I didn't even believe was possible. That is my story.

I took a look at myself, all those years of working so hard 6 days a week, never taking time for myself, because I was too busy pleasing everyone else. I was overweight, menopausal and just plain tired. I needed a reason to move forward. Not just any reason, one with a purpose. So, I started researching why I was such a health train wreck at 50.

I learned about diet and nutrition, hired a personal trainer and started learning about being the healthy woman I wanted to be. My trainer pushed organic foods, healthy eating, and to keep moving. After a year he said to me one day, "If you are eating organic but still using unhealthy bath and body products you are wasting your time because you are still getting the unhealthy chemicals in your body since your skin is your largest organ" So I immediately went to the grocery store and read ingredients and realized he was right. At that time people didn't understand those things about your skin absorbing your bath and body products.

I became obsessed researching and learning all I could about this. I decided after much researching, I would create my own products for personal use, then I thought what if I bought a small company that already made these things I could fast track the progress.

My research leads me to Provincetown Massachusetts and a sweet little company called Provincetown Soap Works. They had amazing products from Shampoos, soaps, lotions and my favorite Lip Balms. It was exactly what I needed. I bought it after 2 visits, spent the time training on how to make everything and the manufacturing practices and moved it to Florida.

It was a bold move. I had the confidence within myself to succeed. I started taking classes all over the US about soap making. Any and all that I could sign up for. I joined the Soap makers Guild to learn about good manufacturing, and took more courses from college professors who were also chemists. It was amazing and very fulfilling.

Working with breast cancer organizations I realized that deodorant was a huge factor in tumors. With much more research, I created a natural deodorant using essential oils that lets you sweat your body's natural detox system without smelling. I tested it on myself and my construction company. Next, I decided to get certified as organic, which was a huge feat that took 9 months and a chemist full time to complete. I did something even big companies wouldn't tackle because of the cost.

My reasoning is that I wanted people to know I am real and passionate about my ingredients. I sign my emails, Susan

Annette, Dream Maker and World Changer. Seriously I believe we can change the health of this world with great bath and body products.

I would create a test recipe, I, who live in the Florida heat would go home after work, put it on and walk 4 miles in the heat. If I came back and smelled BO go to work the next day and add more of this, take out some of that. After about 4 months we got it right. At first, I saved my old antiperspirant for black tie events, I didn't want to sweat and ruin a good dress. After a year I was codependent no more. I threw it in the trash and took my own leap of faith. It works. Now I supply it to organizations who help ladies and men with Cancer for free. Sometimes they cry to know that someone really cares about them when they feel so alone.

One day a dear friend asked me to go to a School Foundation Gala at one of the most beautiful homes I had ever seen. The mission was to help homeless families with children provide school supplies, lunches and dignity for these little souls who didn't have a great beginning. The next day I sent her a 'thank you' box of my products in Lavender, (her home was French chateau). To my amazement she tried them and loved them. Eventually her whole family all men tried the soap and are hooked. When they run out of soap, it is a crisis! They totally get the importance of good bath and body products. She became one of my best friends and today we enjoy sharing so much love and beauty.

Life went on, I continued to be successful in my professional life, but what I found, was that I was living in a way that was like I was looking for a reward for suffering. I didn't really think about it as a reward but I just lived in the way that I thought other people wanted me to and I embraced the down suffering moments.

Then I met a man I thought I truly loved, I learned a lot from him. He taught me I couldn't fix everything for everyone and if I did it doesn't imply that I would be everything that they need or want.

He was just going through a divorce when I met him. He was sad, alone, angry and broke. All he had was a truck and a lot of big dreams. He was a dreamer, but more than that he believed in himself always. I had never met anyone who believed in himself so much. He knew if he worked hard he could have everything he desired. He gave me the confidence to believe that I also could do anything I desired. It was amazing life.

I invested in his dream to have his own building and we would start multiple businesses and they would all be incredible because we had discipline, hard work, honor all the things I was taught as a child. He worked the outside I was the inside. I got everything I ever dreamed of and so did he, he had all the equipment he could ever desire, I had the cars and a beautiful home, great jewelry so many wonderful things. But, I always felt alone and I didn't know why I felt alone or even that I deserved to feel this way.

To pursue his dream, I had to give up part of me. We worked 6 days a week and sometimes 7. Holidays were spent with his family, who I adored, and our employees and their families. Every holiday, we cooked for 100 to 200 people at our shop. We had music and families, great food and great memories.

What was missing? My family. I didn't have the connection with them for so many years, only on the phone. We never had time to drive to North Carolina to visit with my family or take vacations because we were working so much to make the dream life.

I had become Cinderella again, making life great for everyone around me while I was so alone. I had agreed to this life to get what I desired, I didn't go into it blind.

I have to be honest, I wanted to save this man and make him proud of me. It's what I knew, it's what I learned all those years ago. We even started our relationship out with a deal, a business deal of sorts. He had lost everything in his divorce and I had a small business which was doing well. He would help me in my business and I would help him build his retirement back, in return he would be "the best old man I ever had" and if he messed up (by having other women) he would walk away from everything. That was our deal. I believed it to be real.

The day I locked our door at 1:00 in the afternoon after looking up her address and realizing it was only a mile from our shop, seeing his truck in her driveway, I think I was in so much shock I couldn't feel jealousy. I felt numb inside. When they came out of the house, hair disheveled and denying what I was seeing I knew why I felt so alone. I was the one in the dark all the time. I had no idea, until about 5 minutes before, this was even possible. I went back to work and sat in a chair in my office. He came back and, of course, said I didn't see what I thought. I told him, "we had a deal, if I help you make your retirement which we had in spades, he would be the best old man I ever had and if you weren't you'd walk away." His response was, "I lied". That was that. The biggest train wreck in history had just begun and I was in the middle of it, alone, dyeing inside but still alive.

I wanted to run. Run so far that nobody would ever see me again, but I couldn't. We had a big loan at a small bank and 60 employees with families who counted on us to be adults, and then we had all the jobs that needed to be finished. Again, the discipline kicked in and I couldn't remove myself from this situation. I would have to figure out how to survive it because, more than anything, I couldn't let down all those people who counted on us to be responsible.

Of course, we were the talk of the town. I didn't care. There were so many people counting on us and I couldn't let them down, no matter my personal problems. He came back a few times and tried to break me, tried to get me to walk away with personal attacks. He caused so much pain, but he was no match for that father I grew up with. The iron hands and the strong will. I had been through so much worse than this.

So, when he came into my office with others, verbally attacked me, and tried to hurt me with his words and cruelty, I went right back to that line up and waited for my turn with the belt. Silently shaking inside and probably red in the face, but calm as I could be on the outside. I waited for the cruelty to be over. I didn't cry. I was strong. I was taught by the master of pain. He wanted me to walk away and give him the keys to the kingdom we had created. I would wait for him to leave. Only then would I cry, scream, and let it all out. Not in front of him, I couldn't let him see he had gotten to me. I was stronger because I had learned many years ago the fate of not being tough.

As that relationship came to an end, it felt very much like in the movies. The fugitive, the train wreck scene towards the beginning, it seemed to go on forever and ever. That's how my life began to feel, like a never-ending train wreck. I didn't even know that trains would take that long to wreck and now I was living through it. I had everything that I had ever wanted but my life wasn't really the fairytale that I thought it was. I'm pretty sure that everyone around me had actually known what was going on, but I didn't. I was living so deeply within the story; the truth didn't need to come in and interrupt my fairytale until it did. And then, I was divorced.

How I Learned I Had Been Abused

As a Child, My First Inkling

After the train wreck, I had a good friend who suggested I needed to talk to someone a professional. He had gone to this person and was getting some success on personal matters. So, I made an appointment to see a psychiatrist. I was so excited to get to talk to someone about my dilemma that I showed up 2 days early for my appointment. He was very kind and pointed out my mistake.

During these weekly sessions I had some realizations. Number one, the childhood I had had, wasn't really a childhood, it was abuse and I had held it in way too long. It was time to let it all out. Number two, a few months into the sessions, I may be in love with the person who had recommended this council, who had already confessed to our mutual counselor, that he was in love. Oh, thank God. I had found love again. Someone who wanted me for me. Eureka! I had the answer.

In the beginning of that relationship, was scary. We took things very slowly. We had to get to know each other. Of course, I began my old patterns again; he needed fixing, he needed help due to years of being left behind and unappreciated. I am just the girl to fix him. In return, I had an amazing man who I would adore, cherish, and be everything he always wanted in a partner.

Business wise we were a perfect match, head to head, toe to toe we could analyze and figure out any problem. It was amazing and so fulfilling. I was in love again, this time it was going to be even more magical than the last. He was my soulmate.

A few months into it, still learning about each other. We had to be secretive though, a plan our mutual psychiatrist came up with. We had to wait 5 years to be together. He had used this plan before and it worked perfectly. Seriously? This is really happening? I have the man of my dreams and I can't tell anyone or be in public with him? Seriously? Even bigger than that is I agreed to it, with my heart and soul saying run, run, run, get out of here fast, and don't look back. I was so broken I agreed to the terms of the relationship.

Inside I was dying once more. The perfect man with the perfect life and I had to lie to everyone I knew about everything I was doing. I had spent my life trying to be honest with everyone about everything and now I had to go against my soul to be in love? How much more miserable could I be, stuck between two worlds? One of honesty and integrity and the other, of lies and more lies.

It went against everything in my soul to be a part of his life.

I blamed them for my misery. The truth is, it was misery I created myself, by not being true to myself. I needed love, I needed to be loved. I would take any scrap of anything that resembled love because I didn't love myself. As easy as it is to blame someone else, it wasn't them who forced me to be this person, it was me. I am the creator and I created this *love* story. When all it really was, was a desperate attempt to get someone to love me by being who they needed, instead of honoring myself and my needs.

I was so broken I let it be my life. I had given up. I had finally been beaten, and I didn't even have the energy to fight back anymore. So, I would be this girl who lived a lie for the world and had an inside battle with my soul screaming to fight your way back, don't give up.

We did have a lot of fun. We went on great trips and out of town he was funny and incredible. Once home, I was left alone during the day, he could only have lunch with his friends, he only did holidays with his family, and he only did family trips with his family. I was left alone for 10 long years, this was my life.

Every holiday I was at home alone waiting for him to finish his family dinners and gatherings, weddings, Sunday night dinner with his mom; I was left alone. Nine years into it one night, he called me and he said he couldn't talk to me anymore. He gave no reason. This was the 2nd time he had done this. It broke my heart, I was so scared I was really alone now. He was the person I would confide in with all my personal things too. No warning, he just can't talk to me anymore.

I was like a fish out of water, even though this wasn't a real relationship it was all I had and now, it was gone. After a sleepless night,

I decided to take to the road. I drove to a beach in North Carolina, only to decide to drive to the mountains before even getting a room.

Once in the mountains, I found a nice place to stay, spent the days exercising and listening to music. I didn't answer my phone. I just started thinking, how had I gotten into this mess and allowed it to continue for so long? What could I do to fix my life? How could I create the life I wanted? I had to be smarter than this. What could I do?

In the meantime, he was calling and texting. For a few days I didn't answer. I had to figure out myself first, make a plan. I finally answered after he became very angry. Long story short, I asked if there was someone else he was seeing? I didn't understand at all what had happened to us and why we couldn't talk or text for a week. His explanation was that our psychiatrist hold told him that if he stopped talking to me, he could get me to do anything. He could control me if he scared me enough. Wow, that was my story then.

I made a plan. I would go home and get a new person to talk to and he would help me find myself, set boundaries and become who I knew I was deep down inside. I had a plan, after all these years of suffering in silence. I had a plan. The next year of my life, I would work on me, not anyone else. And that's just what I did.

I loved this man with every cell of my body and he loved me as well. The problem was, we were both broken from things in our childhood, and that was our story. We didn't know how to change it or that we even could. He was told he was stupid and would never amount to anything, which was a complete lie, and I was made to be a soldier and conform to whatever anyone wanted me to be.

All these things were lies we were told and we believed them so much so we took them into our adulthood and into everything we did. Did he intend to hurt me? No way, it's just we didn't know any better, we only knew what we were taught. After I finally got away I would fall in love one more time with yet another amazing man and go as far as to get engaged this time. At the end I knew I couldn't marry this man, I really loved someone else deep inside. It wasn't fair to him.

And the love of my life? Well he met someone else right after I told him I couldn't marry him, and asked her to marry him and they started a beautiful life with family and friends and a new home and everything I had dreamed of with him for 10 long years, she was living the life I wanted for us, my life.

I decided then and there that I would find a way out of this life I had created. I would take responsibility and create something I deserved. Something real, where I could really be me and be honest.

That fateful night I had broken off with yet another great man and lay in bed crying and hurting. Crying and yelling and miserable beyond all misery, wishing I could end it right now. I realized then that I was really in love with my soulmate and he was gone to another life, with a new wife, and never to give me a chance to show him I could be the one. I decided to give it all up and end the endless pain of trying to be loved by someone else. The girl who loved to be loved had run her course, it wasn't meant to be. She could find the amazing, talented, smart, incredible men one after the other, but it was me who was broken.

You see I was trained to make people happy, to give all of myself. However, I wasn't trained how to be myself, genuinely, out loud if you will. I was trained to be an imposter. The chameleon. Nobody really wants that. It always ends badly. So, this weekend, I would make it final, once and for all.

He hadn't done anything wrong in fact he was everything I wanted; handsome, smart, retired, happy, lots of fun, he liked to travel, we had a good time. We went on diets together, the beach on weekends, spent time with friends, he made me laugh out loud so easily. He was truly amazing and everything a girl could ask for.

It was me, I just wasn't happy and I felt like it wasn't really right, more to the point I wasn't right. I did not have myself together enough to make this work, I hadn't grown myself enough. I was still being the chameleon, and you know, he had every right to know the real me, which I hid to be with him. I didn't even know how to tell him how I felt. I wasn't being really myself yet and I didn't want to end another marriage in divorce. I needed to stay married, more importantly happily married.

That night, I was so lost and alone, thinking, "what was thinking? The man of my dreams and I had broken up with him." He was devastated, hurt, and angry. He didn't understand. Neither did I.

It was Friday night, I was crying out of control, lying in bed thinking I'll do it this time, I'll kill myself by Sunday. I'll spend the weekend getting everything in order. I just couldn't get it right and I was so lost and sick about my actions. I was so sad and wished I could just be put out my misery now. Nobody will miss me, they all know what a messed-up loser I really am. I'm never satisfied enough with me. It'll be for the best. I'll make sure everyone is taken care of financially and it'll be easy for everyone to move on. This time I'll do it, how am I going to get through this night though I am so lost inside?

Then I looked over at the fireplace and saw that book I had given him, I had hoped he could use to find his peace, but he never opened it. I picked it up and I opened it randomly to page 86. It read "Express Service" by Mike Dooley. Crying and wondering how I was ever going to ever stop crying or even get to sleep, I started reading the page, and there they were. The secret words I had searched for most of my life. The peace and courage I needed to live, to be the Susan that was real and followed her inner voice, her peace, her nature.

It wasn't just words, it was more. I read it over, and over, and over, until I stopped crying and I started smiling. Right there in that moment, my old life stopped, and I started living. I understood that I was not alone, not now, not ever. It wasn't real, what I was searching for. Real love was inside me, it always had been, I just didn't know it.

I am not alone, I never was and sitting there high atop a stand at the train station watching people come and go and seeing the beautiful lives they are living and wondering if my life was passing me by. I turn and see a kindly old soul sitting beside me in the comfort of my own first-class cabin and she smile and said to me, you are not alone, your train will come and you will know it and begin your own journey just as you planned it long ago. Then I started the real plan.

Being true to myself, a journey that would take a few years but was so worth it. I became the love of my life, the girl who loved too much finally loved herself. I made myself a promise, I would never break my own heart again.

Yes, I had that power and I had that control now. I could find love outside myself, but I didn't *need* that to complete me. I was already complete just being me and loving me. I will always be the girl who loved too much. The difference is, I love myself just as much.

I will get a good night's sleep and in the morning, I would find out where this guy was speaking and I was going there, no matter where it was, the next speaking engagement I was going to be there, and I was.

The next 4 years I learned about me. Not anyone else, just me and how I could be the person I always dreamed I would be. The girl who loved herself without conditions, the girl who forgave those people who hurt her without conditions. I grew my heart so big I was so happy and it was real, not a fad, it is real. That is how my story began.

Learning to Love Myself Like I wanted to be Loved.

My Soul was talking to me, she said, "I gave up too much of myself to be with others". They didn't let me be me, and even worse, I didn't let me be me. I wasn't real. I wasn't genuine. I thought if I was really me, who would want me? If I was real and asked for what I wanted and needed they wouldn't love me. So I would give up my real self to be who they needed, who they could love.

I couldn't trust them to leave them alone for the weekend if I visited my family. Why? Because I wasn't listening to my soul, she told me they weren't right for me, they weren't honest. I wanted them anyway, for something they could give me, love. The love I had all along I just didn't tap into it. As a result, I became whatever they loved, not what I loved. I didn't love me enough to be myself. Like I wasn't worthy of being me. If I had loved myself enough to be me, they may have still loved me, I just couldn't take that chance.

I was ashamed of myself for no good reason. If I only loved me like I deserved then, I probably could have saved my relationships. At least one or two of them. I truly loved these guys and I believe they loved me, but they really didn't get to know the real me, the genuine me. If they did would they still love me? Who knows?

I agreed and changed myself without asking is that really what you want? Sometimes I would say "It's ok, I can do this. I can go without music, I can go without TV, I don't need to see my family on holidays or birthdays, I don't need to go socialize with my friends, it isn't that much to give up for love". Then again, why do I have to give up anything for love? That should have been my question why do I have to give up anything for love?

I love music like no one you know. At sister weekends we have theme songs. They all do submissions and I pick our song. I love music, soft, happy, country, pop, rock, all kinds of music. It pleases my soul to dance and smile like no one is watching. Why would I give up such a beautiful part of myself to receive love?

OMG suddenly I was at peace, the answer was there. All I have to do is listen, be still and the answers will come. I read it again, put the book down and knew in the morning I would find this author and see him in person. He saved my life, or actually I saved my life by listening to my soul.

When I told him, he saved my life he said I saved myself. I replied no you saved me and he said again, you saved yourself. I didn't get it yet. Now I know that is true. It would take a little while longer for me to get that part of it. All I knew was I wasn't desperate for love anymore because I have all the love I need, right here inside me. I just needed to remember that.

Open Your Heart and Open Your Mind

Opening your heart and mind gives you a chance to know the real you, not the you the world and your parents told you to be. The genuine you who has ideas on how your real life can be. Obviously, you aren't happy with your life now or you wouldn't be reading this book.

So, if you could have anything you wanted and be anything, why not create that for yourself?

If you want to be loved unconditionally, completely, with honor and honesty why not start that this second by loving yourself that way? What are you waiting for? If you want that then do it. You have the power to say right now wherever you are, "I love myself just like I want to be loved, unconditionally without judgment or criticism."

Love yourself like that, it's easy, it's free, you don't even have to make a move off your sofa or chair. Just begin to love you like you would like to be loved. Stop right now! Imagine the love you have for yourself, without judgment. I say this over and over because we judge ourselves many times a day. You know all the things you say, you're not smart enough, thin enough, young enough…on and on and on. What if for just today, this minute, this second you stop everything else you are doing and take 5 minutes to talk to yourself like you would the person you admire most in your life?

Why don't you become the person you admire most? The person who overcome all odds to love themselves? Forgive yourself for all the mistakes you've made and for anything you have done. You have the power to forgive yourself right now. A new beginning with you becoming the star of your own show. The person you were meant to be. You can become the love of your life. It's just the beginning of the beautiful journey you can be on if you open your heart and mind.

You have the most beautiful soul inside you. Your soul is always there with you, guiding you, loving you, and always wishing the best for you. You may have suppressed them and stopped listening to your soul long ago. Listen to your soul, it loves you like you deserve to be loved.

You are never alone, never. When I have my worst days, somehow some way my soul speaks to me, "open that book, look at that contract again." She is always guiding me gently and with love. She sends me the thoughts that I need to do something. Like to write this book to help others find their own love and peace. It's subtle, but if you listen you can begin to create the reality you really want and deserve.

You know, the universal language is love. The universe has more love than any of us can ever use, more than we could even imagine and it is available to everyone. Every nanosecond for eternity. You can tap into it anytime you wish or desire. It's your choice to begin this journey and I hope with all my heart that you will take a leap of faith and start right now. Right this second.

The only thing you have to lose is the bad parts of your life. Open your heart and your mind and watch love flow through you, to you and around you. I can see it, and feel it. Can you?

Make a promise to yourself, "I will not break my own heart again and I will not let others break me. I love myself and I will protect myself from pain, I give myself unconditional love now and forever."

Too Much Past and Not Enough

Present

Easy to say, more challenging to do, isn't it? Notice I didn't say "hard" to do. I didn't for a reason, why put that out there? Let's put out there what we intend on happening instead of what is happening and change it to what we want to happen.

Well the whole point of this is to create the thinking that propels you forward in love. As one of my friends loves to say "Forward in Grace".

Looking backward is to learn life lessons. It is a time of your life that doesn't have to really be anymore. It was a life lesson not a life sentence. I've looked back many times and really think about the situation, like an observation.

I fell in love with someone driving over a bridge. It was an ah-ha moment for sure. One side of the bridge I was just me going to the bank to make my daily deposit, and at the top of the bridge I felt a shift. Then, while driving down the other side, was like slow motion. I realized I was in love, just like that. Ten years later I was still in love.

Two years before I had given up on my soul mate, if he were to ever ask me to marry him, I realized I had to say no. It was heartbreaking, also bottoming out I knew I had to fix me to move forward.

So, I spent a year in therapy working on myself, getting happy again, loving myself for once. Then I took the leap out of his life and into my own. I lived in the beautiful house I had built, I watched moon rises, I lived for once.

As I was driving over the same bridge yesterday I was thinking about the love story with him and I realized one year after I left he was in love with someone else, engaged, married and building the house of his dreams for them, not us the us I wanted to be. Then I felt embarrassed that I didn't get all that. I said to myself, it's ok because he didn't change, I did. What I intended by this was that he is still the same guy that I was with and that wasn't what I really needed. He was the person I had the most in common with, but it was really one sided. He controlled me with the love I had for him. It wasn't equal love. He was nice to me, I just never felt real love, like I was the best thing in his life.

In fact, I was 4th in line for his affections. After his mom, sister and son. I was the 4th person to get attention. Always left behind. Nothing I could do would get me to first. When I left, he did a lot of things to get me back, including asking me to forgive him for leaving me behind for so long. I wasn't ready yet, I couldn't trust him because I didn't really believe he had changed. Just like that, he moved on to the next girl. Not giving me a chance like I had given him all those years to find my way to forgiveness.

So yes, I was embarrassed briefly, but I couldn't close the deal. Yes, so far, he is the love of my life. You love your abusers. Looking back lets me see what I need to run from, as fast as possible. Moving forward is your only option if you want to have a happy life. There are millions of men in this world. If only 1% of them are right for me then there are at least a million who would love me.

Break it down and you will see it is better to wait than to live in constant misery. This isn't my story anymore, I have a more beautiful story brewing right now in my heart and soul and it's about equals, love and happiness. Learning and living out loud. It is my newest story and I love it completely.

"The only thing that is real in life is the step you are taking right now." Eckart Tolley

My Message is About Love

My message for you is about love, love for yourself unconditionally. Exactly how you would like to be loved. You can love yourself like this, how? It's easy really. Think about something you really love, babies, chocolate cake, amazing cars, football whatever it is that you adore. Simply sit and think about this thing you love so much, maybe a person, your child, your parents, your friend whatever it is. Think about the thing you love so much, feel the happiness, feel the love in your heart, feel the happiness of your brain. That is real love. That feeling.

Now, imagine you love yourself like that, feel yourself love yourself in the place of the image you have. That is how you begin to love yourself, you should love yourself as much as or more than anything else you can think of.

Begin loving yourself like you want to be loved and your whole world will shift, you shift, you change your life story, everything in your life responds to love, you respond to love. Feel that feeling even a small amount will begin your journey. The journey of love.

Love is the universal language; a smile is universal. Smile about how much you can love yourself without judgment.

IF You Really Believe in You, Everyone Else Will Too

You can unplug from massive conscience and create a separate reality.

I have a dream of how I would love my life to be right now, no more waiting. I want to be the girl who talks you into dipping your toes into the wealth of universal love and power that is available to all of us, where abundance, love and happiness are unlimited.

Where all you have to do is believe with faith as small as a mustard seed, that's all. That and more can be yours, right now, at this very moment. It only takes faith. Faith in yourself that with all your stories and all your perceived flaws, you deserve the best life has to offer.

Turn yourself around literally, like the Hokey Pokey. Stand up and turn yourself around. When you do, pretend you have everything you desire and beyond. Imagination is limitless. Look at JK Rowling. I often wonder how she created that whole world of Harry Potter. Unlimited imagination, she opened herself to herself and let it flow.

In the mornings, I get up early, make a cup of coffee, and sit. Listening to alternative music and letting the creativity flow. Sometimes I think of things and I begin to write. A few days later I will look at what I have written and it's like I am seeing it for the first time. At first, I thought I was losing my memory then I realized I am at one with my soul and the things I already knew. When I am quiet it flows from me much like your heart beating, it's always there you just have to acknowledge it. Take a sabbatical and listen to your soul guide you, remind you, enlighten you, and show you love. The love you require is always within you, always.

When I was a child I had these things always going on in my mind, way in the back. Thoughts I had never told anyone. Number one was that I was going to own my own business. For as long as I can remember I knew this. I have owned many businesses and they have all been amazing. I wanted a rich father who would love me and just before turning 21, I met for the first time, my real father. He was very wealthy and kind. Just like I imagined and more. He owned many businesses and was really a great businessman.

Now how can a 6-year-old visualize these things and they come true? Because they are always inside you. I never knew what kind of business and I never really tried to narrow it down, I let that flow naturally.

The point of all this is, listen to your thoughts, the things you know are real, not the ones who say, you are too fat or too short or not smart enough. Weed out those thoughts and focus on the positive ones.

Energy flows where attention goes. That's very important, so I'll say it again, energy flows where attention goes. Don't let yourself undermine yourself with negative energy. We were born to succeed and to make the life we desire. The bumps and bruises along the way are just temporary stories. They don't have to be your real story unless you require them to be. Unless you can build upon them to your mega story. The one where you prevail against all odds and become the beautiful, amazing, kind caring soul you were always meant to be.

This can be your story, it's only a thought away, was always only a thought away. "If you really believe in you, everyone else will too."

Childhood, Something You Spend Your Whole Life Getting Over

Sometimes the things that happened are too much for a young mind to handle and they are scarred for life. Or they just don't know you can change your life, your story, your future.

You never know what someone has been through. Their perception, their pain, their hurt. That's why judging someone on their outward actions becomes self-serving, we don't know what everyone went through. Maybe it was good, maybe not.

Always remember, abuse is abuse no matter the form and it can take a lifetime to see that it was just a small part of your life.

Although, the most important informative years, but not your life story. It can be anything you can imagine it is a choice. In my own case I didn't even know I was physically abused, because I believed it was normal behavior to beat your child to the point of going to an emergency room. I thought I was that bad of a girl. I was 40 years old before someone told me that wasn't normal.

I always hid my body because of the bruising. Once I knew that was a thing I started living that story, but I also started noticing how I let many people control me, take advantage of me, use me and abuse me without saying anything. That was my training.

Once I started resisting and changing myself, people started falling out of my life. Really good people, close friends, family it was scary at first and I wondered what am I doing wrong? How can I lose these people? Then I realized once I was able to stand up for me, they run away because they are the abusers. They need others to abuse and control. Once I was strong enough to not be the doormat anymore, to stop giving my power, my love, my everything to them, they went on with their lives without me in it.

Was it painful? Of course, some of them were my longer relationships in my life. Now I see quicker when I am being used and when I am being appreciated. Yes, I still let users in, because as someone once told me, we all get something out of relationships. Sometimes we just love so much we look over those things that are uncomfortable.

Judging everyone is a full-time job. One which I don't have the time for anymore. If I were to waste my time judging everyone else, there is no time for me to heal and advance my own self. I am not the sum of what everyone else thinks I am, I am what I think I am. I am genuine and true as I can be and I spend a lot of time reading and learning ways to be even more genuine and true, and not worry about what others have to say.

As long as you are growing, someone is going to try to hold you back by questioning your intentions. Intentions are personal. I believe we are all a work in progress, and maybe I am weak because I question authenticity of many things, beliefs, messages. However, there is nothing wrong with being weak, the wrong is in thinking you know everything so much that you are not open to differences.

I have a friend who asks you a question as a conversation started and you get to answer it with a quick answer and then she uses it to talk forever on how much she knows about the subject. She knows everything about everything and you listen and listen and think her mind is really closed up. She already knows everything there is no room for new knowledge from others. Her whole circle is like this, they pride themselves on how smart they are.

One of the sayings I love is "Nobody cares how much you know, until they know how much you care." And why is being smart so important? Questioning is innocence to me, it opens the doors to possibilities and new answers that have not even been thought of, maybe.

We all have insecurities and beliefs, in my case I believe we should be open to all the possibilities all the ideas. All the knowledge and not limits to just what we think we know.

The Girl Who Loves Too Much,

What I Learned

I have dated a few times. This time with eyes wide open. If at dinner they are looking at their cell phone or watching beautiful women walk by our table, or anything else that isn't what I require, I stop the interest. I stop it right there in its tracks.

No longer willing to settle, or be a settler no longer will I stop acknowledging what I feel inside. I will no longer be the chameleon. I will be me. I will always be the girl who loved too much, but I will never be the girl who gave up being herself to make someone else happy. I will be the girl who loves herself enough not to break her own heart and the girl who will not give anyone else that power.

By conforming myself and compromising who I was just to be loved or to feel like I was being loved. It was through this journey that I was able to develop the ability to really help things that I've used with many people to help them go through their own journey to remove themselves from the story that they're living in and change it. I applied what I did myself and for many others and here is what I've learned.

1. You have to begin to change your story. So first you need to ask yourself, what is the story that you're basing your life on?

    My friend, when she was a little kid, her parents abused her. They pulled her pigtails and told her she was ugly and fat, all things that are very traumatic for a little girl. They adored her sister but they didn't like her. She has now been married for 38 years to the same guy, they have four beautiful children who adore her. They have every holiday with their children. You know, it's a family unit. She has grandchildren that adore her. Her life is beautiful now. But, the only thing she can think about is that little girl who got abused.

I encouraged her like I am encouraging you now. How long was your childhood? I mean, mine was only 16 years and then after that, it's a whole other life. She has to be grateful for the life she has now, and not focus on that small portion of her life anymore. We all have a story and sometimes it's awful but as we begin to look at it, what we have to realize is how long ago that was. We're not enjoying the life now because of the story from back then and that is a true tragedy.

2. Realize how long you have been defining yourself by this story.

   I remember talking to my friend and sharing with her and as we begin to talk about the fact that the story she had defined for herself, was when she was a child, she had to remember that 30 or 40 years had gone by and she was still allowing what had happened back then to be the definition of what she let happen now. When we begin to realize how long ago that story is, then we can release ourselves from that and can move forward.

3. Forgive the story, the person, the incident, whatever it is.

Forgiveness isn't for them, it's for you, and by doing that we release ourselves from that story and make an opportunity to write a new story and to change the way our life is, because we change our story.

4. We realize all the gifts that we've been given in life since the time of that story.

Again, with my friend, she realized she had her beautiful children and how wonderful it had been being their mom and all of the gifts that had come along with that. As well as many of the things in her life. By really taking note of the gifts that we have in life, the opportunities, the things that we've accomplished, we're able to change our story.

5. Lastly, by realizing that that story is over, we can then begin to ask ourselves, "What do you want your story to be?"

For me, I knew that I would no longer was desperate to find someone to love me. That there had been that whole life that had gone by since that story and that I can change my story. I didn't have to be the hurt person anymore.

All of us have tons of stories as we go through our lifetime, but what we can do is take control of the ones that are the stories we want to live by. So, you look at people like Wayne Dyer, or Steve Jobs, many of them are people who have been broke or broken, often homeless, sometimes even without parents. They've been through things to.

I will love again, this time someone who loves themselves and who loves me just like I am. With my perceived flaws and all. (Always working on that) Someone who is whole all by themselves and wants someone in their life that is also whole. It isn't a competition, it is love.

One more thing I've also learned is that childhood is what you spend your whole life getting over. Sometimes any little reminder of those traumas puts you right back into being a little child. One of my great loves and I would cook together. He would always make my portion much smaller than his, it was so obvious I felt uncomfortable to the point I would look away while he would fill his plate and then I would get what was left. It put me right back into my childhood with my father who allowed us one cookie while he sat in front of us eating the whole bag, one by one.

Once he was really upset about something and I was so scared, I was right back to that lineup, sweating, trying to be still and silent. It was a defining moment for me. I promised myself I would never be scared in my own home again, by anyone, ever. I learned love is a partnership, it is two people who love each other equally.

While cleaning out old photographs and old cards I found one for my husband for Valentine's Day. I had signed it all those years ago, "I love you more". I wouldn't know how true that was until many years later. I loved him with my whole heart and I was willing to give up my life to make his what he had dreamed. I was willing to do anything, work 6 days a week, ignore my own family, forget about vacations, anything he wanted I would do, just to make him happy.

The truth was nothing I could do would make him totally happy because he needed the thrill of chasing new girls and conquering them because that is how he was taught.

No loyalty to anyone including himself. Did he love me, yes, he did because I was willing to give my all and all he has to do is take. I created that dynamic and who wouldn't love that? I learned then that if you aren't happy already, nobody else can complete you or make you happy. Happiness is an inside job.

Here we go down the path to peace and happiness, it's all just a thought away. Let's do this together and begin the journey to love, light and happiness. If you begin to open your mind and your heart, if you awaken yourself, you cannot go back to your limited beliefs anymore. So right now, right here, is your beginning and there is no turning around. You need to be ready to make this shift and move forward. I will show you the way, it's my job to show you there is more than enough love in this world and you hold the key, you always have.

I encourage you to take some time, choose happiness over suffering, write down the life that you want to create for yourself, ask yourself why am I suffering? Then decide that you're not going to suffer anymore. Write down what your life would look like if you had the story that you want.

For me, it had to do with having the people in my life that were really truly my friends, equal friendships and now I get to go out and have girl's night with them. We have sleepovers with each other, we have charities events, small or big ones even with 200 to 300 people. I know now, that I want to be loved but I don't need to be disingenuous to get that love anymore. That there is a person for me to love and it's okay to be me and look for that person who loves me as me.

You don't have to be perfect, you don't have to take care of everyone you meet. It's okay to love yourself first and to love yourself unconditionally. I encourage you to take this commitment on for yourself and to decide that from now on, that you won't break your heart by loving people that are not right for you. That you'll take responsibility for your life. Far too often, we have that feeling in our gut that tells us that something's wrong. I encourage you, listen to it.

Love yourself. Don't break your own heart. Remember that there's no reward for suffering and most importantly, that you can change your story. Happiness is an inside job, and even though you may have heard that phrase before, I hope that you'll take it internally this time and know that what you really want in life, is not a reward for suffering but rather happiness. That's the reward you're seeking. I love that the universe now has given me a place to be able to share this truth. There is an abundance of love for everyone. We all deserve goodness. I know of all the things that I've been through, and of all the stories that have been in in my life, they are now in the past. That I have the power to change my story and that through that I can now help you, to change your story.

I learned no matter how hard I wished it, I am not going to be friends with everyone. Some people are going to look at me and say she isn't a normal person, she has more, she thinks more, she questions more, she requires more, she isn't religious enough for us. I believe in thanking God and the universe for all of our gifts and that a piece of God lives inside each of us. I believe we are God. I believe in happiness, love and kindness and I believe we all deserve good and that anyone can change their life to the one of their dreams if they just believe that.

I believe being thankful for your blessings is a very powerful way to start the day, and if you can have the faith the size of a mustard seed you can change your life and change your story to the one of your dreams. Life is but a dream and my dreams are to be eternally happy, healthy, wealthy and wise. Forgive and forget, live and love, and most of all be kind to everyone without judgment of their journey. I pray to God and the universe that I have the strength to accomplish all these things in my lifetime and to help as many other people as I can, to see this light as well. I believe it is my journey to open your mind to the love and light that is ours for the opening of our minds.

Depression is living in the past, we are all given a gift it is called the "Present". Open your gift as soon as you can.

With love and light, Life is but a dream.

Susan